A Note from Sylvia Woods
from Kauai, Hawaii

Lava is a short film that was released and shown with the Disney-Pixar Inside Out movie in the summer of 2015. It is the story of a volcano who has waited millions of years for his one true "lava." This song, which tells the story throughout the short, was written by the film's director.

The four verses and very similar to each other, with minor note and rhythm changes to match the lyrics. The same is true for the four choruses. Since it can sound a bit repetitious, you might decide to shorten the arrangement if you are playing it as a harp solo, without the lyrics. If you would like to do this, I suggest you leave out one or two of the middle verses and choruses, and then finish with Verse 4 (on page 7) and Chorus 4 to the end. I have marked the beginning of each verse and chorus in the music to help you easily find them.

This music can be played on harps with just one octave below middle C. The range needed is 3 octaves (22 strings) from C to C. No sharping levers are required.

Unfortunately, there is not much time to make the page turns. I apologize for this. When necessary, you can leave out some of the left hand notes, or play them with the right hand, to facilitate turning the page.

In the movie, this song is accompanied by a Hawaiian ukulele. I've tried to simulate this sound in this arrangement.

Whenever the following left hand pattern appears, I suggest that you only place fingers 4 and 2. Then, after you play 4 and 2, lift your hand and place the 2 and 1. This will give the same bouncy feel as the other measures. You could also finger the first two notes as 3 and 1, instead of 4 and 2, if you prefer.

And here's a bit of movie trivia for you. The male volcano's name is Uku, and the female is Lele!

Aloha and mahalo (thank you),

Sylvia Woods

LAVA

To simulate the sound of a ukulele, all the notes of the chords should be played together;
do not arpeggiate them, except where marked.

Music and Lyrics by James Ford Murphy

Harp Arrangement by Sylvia Woods

Easy half-time feel

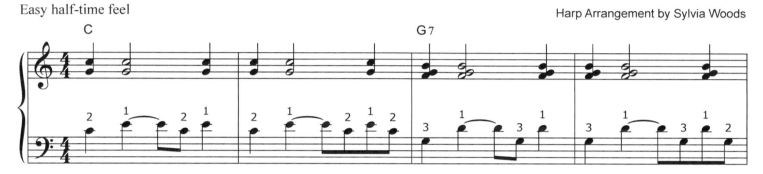

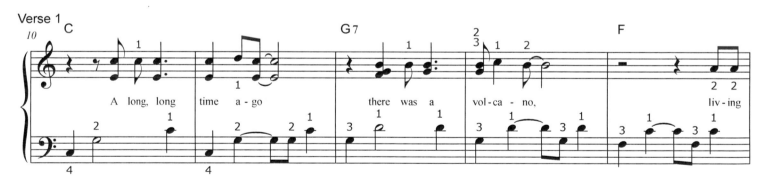

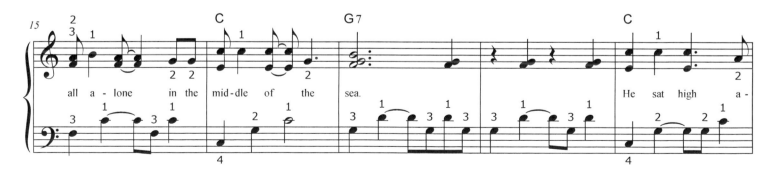

bove his bay, watch-ing all the cou-ples play, and wish-ing that

he had some-one too. And from his la-va came this

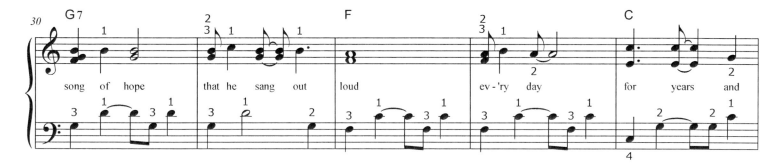

song of hope that he sang out loud ev-'ry day for years and

years. Chorus 1 F "I have a dream I hope will come

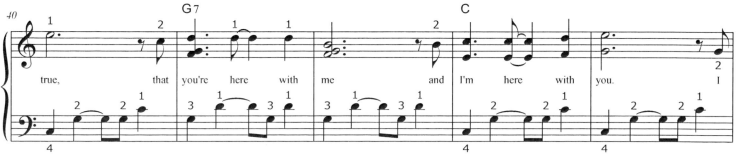

true, that you're here with me and I'm here with you. I

The last 2 or 3 LH notes may be omitted
or played with the right hand for page turn

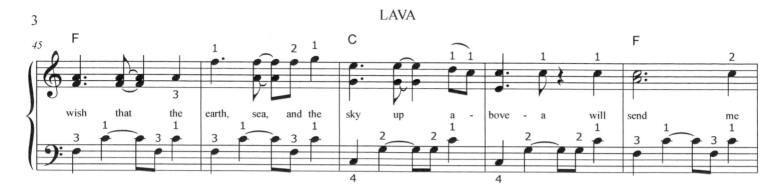

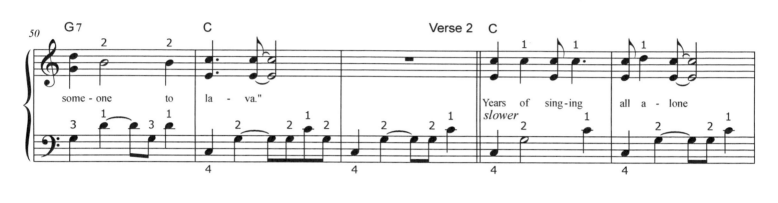

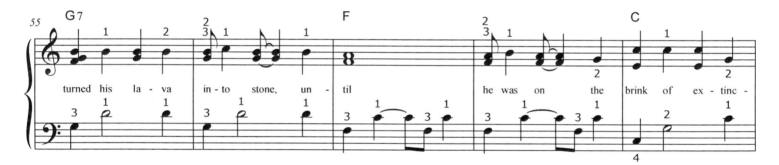

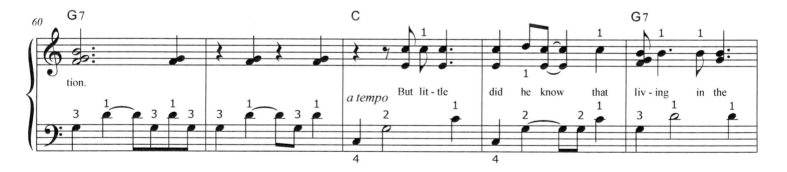

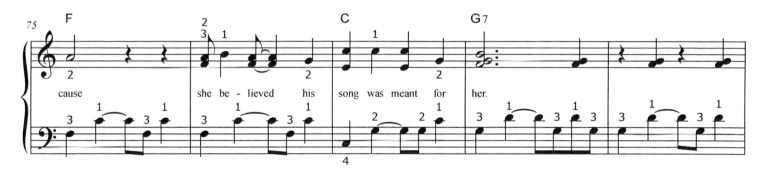

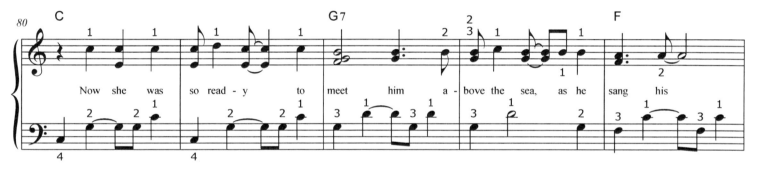

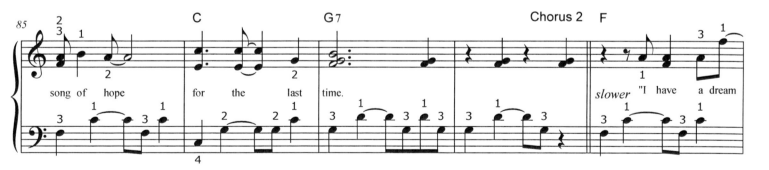

The last 2 or 3 LH notes may be omitted
or played with the right hand for page turn

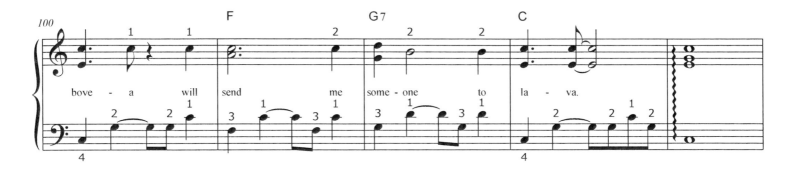

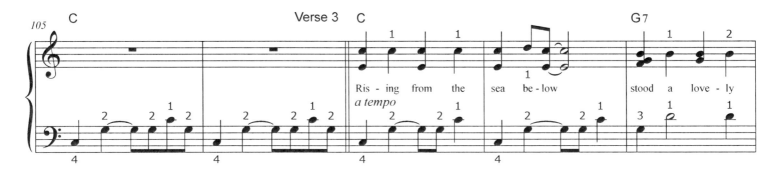

with no   la - va his   song was all   gone.   He
slower

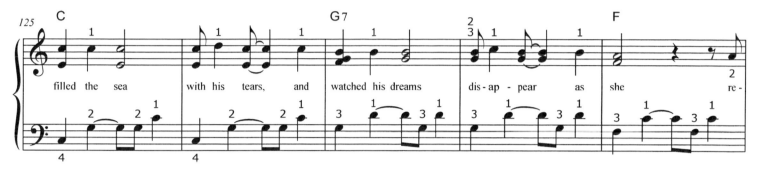

filled the sea   with his tears, and   watched his dreams   dis - ap - pear as   she   re -

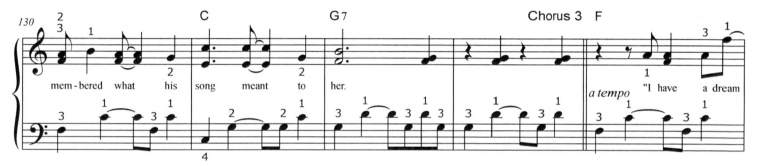

mem - bered what his   song meant to   her.   *a tempo* "I have a dream

Chorus 3   F

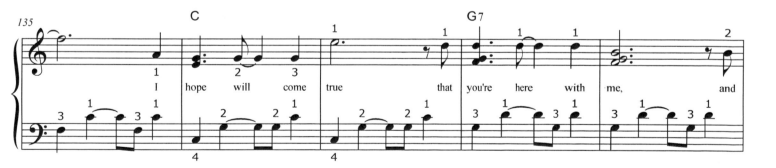

I   hope will come   true   that you're here with   me,   and

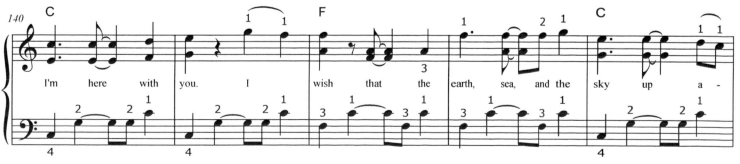

I'm here with you.   I   wish that the   earth, sea, and the   sky up a -

The last 2 or 3 LH notes may
be omitted for page turn

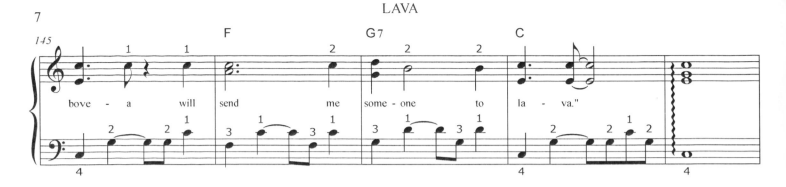

bove - a will send me some-one to la - va."

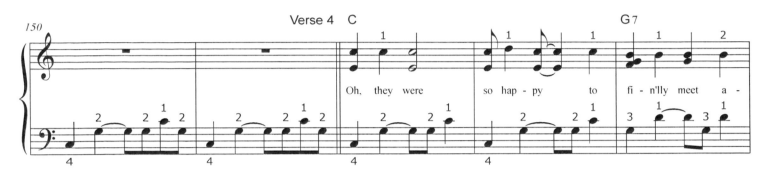

Verse 4

Oh, they were so hap-py to fi-n'lly meet a-

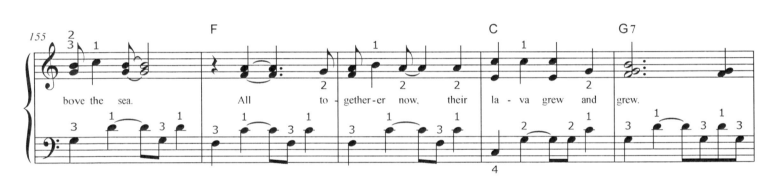

bove the sea. All to-gether-er now, their la - va grew and grew.

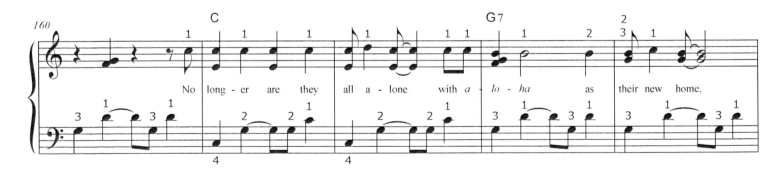

No long-er are they all a-lone with a-lo-ha as their new home,

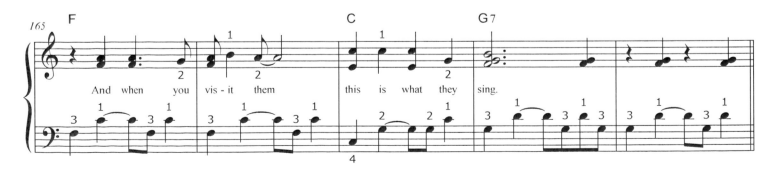

And when you vis-it them this is what they sing.